Getting Started In Wildlife Rehabilitation

By Ame Vanorio

Ame Vanorio

Dedication: To Big Buddy and Little Buddy, my first rehabilitation raccoons. You taught me so much about love and letting go with joy.

Contents

Introduction to This Series

This book is <u>Volume 1</u> and is geared to giving you a comprehensive overview of wildlife rehabilitation including the business side of things, skills and training, supplies you need, and learning the basics on administering fluids, transportation, triage, warmth, and so much more.

<u>Volume 2</u> (coming May 2023) will deal with all the diseases, parasites, infections, and wounds that the wildlife may come with into your home or center. We will talk about treatment options, things you can do, and when to call a vet.

<u>Volume 3</u> (coming June 2023) will break down individual species, give a treatment plan, feeding schedule, and what specific needs they may have.

What is Wildlife Rehabilitation?

Wildlife rehabilitation is the rescue and care of injured and orphaned wildlife. Wildlife rehabilitators play an important role as conservationists and humanitarians.

Primarily this focuses on neonates and baby wildlife, but it may also include juveniles and adults. The goal of rehabilitation is to put the animal back into the wild when it's ready to live on its own.

Wildlife Rehabilitators play an important role as conservationists and humanitarians. Rescued wildlife often have human inflicted injuries that may be caused by being hit by a car or lawnmower, the parents being trapped or shot, or habitat destruction.

They may be displaced or injured due to floods and fires occurring in their habitat.

The rehabilitator provides medical care, feeding, as well as natural experiences so that animals can be returned to their native environment. They arrange for veterinary care and provide appropriate housing.

The National Wildlife Rehabilitation Association defines wildlife rehabilitation *as the professional care given to sick, injured, and orphaned wild animals with the ultimate goal of having them be returned to their natural habitat.*

Why I Got into Wildlife Rehab...

I have loved animals my whole life and was lucky enough to grow up on a farm where we had lots of pets, horses, and livestock. I grew up in the 1970s and early '80s before wildlife rehabilitation laws existed.

People were always bringing me wild and domestic animals that had been hurt or orphaned. My parents had a wonderful vet who was always willing to give me guidance and help me with my "babies". In high school I spent many Saturdays going on farm calls with him as his helper.

During college I worked for the National Wildlife Federation teaching wildlife conservation and Environmental Education.

I became a science and special education teacher and doing vet assistant work on the side. It was only a matter of time before that morphed into becoming a licensed wildlife rehabilitator. At that time Fox Run Environmental Education Center became a non-profit and I was rehabbing 100 – 150 babies per year.

We desperately need more wildlife rehabilitators across the United States! As a rehabber, you can take on as few or as many animals as you are able. You do not have to accept any animal you are not comfortable with taking on. Some people specialize in one or two species, and some are open to many.

Understandably many people do not have the time and/or money it takes to rehab. In that case, there are many other ways you can support your local rehabber. Volunteer, donate money, or something from their need list, and share their posts on social media.

WHY DOES WILDLIFE NEED TO BE REHABILITATED?

Research shows that the majority of injured, ill, and orphaned wild animals handled by rehabilitators are suffering not because of "natural" occurrences, but because of human intervention -- some accidental, some intentional, many preventable. Injuries due to cars, mowers, firearms, traps, kids throwing stones, poisons, oil spills, pets, can be life-threatening.

Rehabilitators treat injuries in these animals by either caring for them until they can be released or having them humanely euthanized.

Rehabbers seek to educate the public on how to prevent these problems and work with citizens having wildlife/human conflicts. Some wildlife rehabilitators conduct education programs for the public. They may have USDA qualified education animals that are non-releasable and bring them to community classes.

THEY ARE NOT PETS

Wildlife rehabilitation is not an attempt to turn wild animals into pets. Animals remain in captivity only until they are able to live independently in the wild and then they are released. In fact, we have minimal contact with our babies. It's important that they develop appropriate fear of humans, dogs, and cats in order for them to survive.

Wild animals do not make good pets. In addition, it is against the law to possess a wild animal in many other states without a permit. Often states impose fines or jail time for not abiding by wildlife laws. Sadly, what sometimes happens is that Fish and Wildlife or DNR officers kill the animal on the spot.

What Skills Do Wildlife Rehabilitators Need?

In many ways, wildlife rehabilitators are like nurses. We provide medical care to distressed animals. Animals in need of rescue come to us with injuries, separation anxiety, and parasites.

For the most part, these animals are not happy or healthy. They are in crisis.

An important part of your job is compassion for both the animal and the finder. Finders often make mistakes and need education and guidance.

Wildlife rehabilitation is not a solitary job (sorry!). Working with the public and providing a calm resource when they are panicking or need some helpful advice due to a nuisance issue such as squirrels living in the attic or foxes killing chickens.

Along with compassion, a good rehabber has a working knowledge of first aid and triage. Wildlife Rehabbers work with a veterinarian to establish good medical practices. And most important, for their safety and the animal's well-being rehabbers need to have an understanding of zoonoses - animal to people diseases.

In addition, wildlife rehabbers often need to be skilled in basic carpentry or have volunteers that are to design and build appropriate enclosures. Having a good understanding of the species' habitat is important and you need to manage all that waste.

According to the International Wildlife Rehabilitation Council, on average, rehabilitators can expect to spend 35% of their time caring for animals, 35% working with the public, 15% handling administrative tasks, and 15% managing the facility.

SKILLS YOU NEED

- Administer fluids
- Give injections
- Wound care
- Basic body evaluation with temperature, weight, and skin condition
- Humane restraint and capture strategies
- Knowledge of providing a safe and clean enclosure
- Knowledge of feeding and nutrition for the species under your care
- Ability to perform humane euthanasia
- Dealing with people on the phone
- Carpentry skills to build enclosures

PASSION

My personal belief is along with skills you must have passion.

Do you stop and pull over to help a turtle cross the road?

Do you lead a neighborhood search to help find a lost pet?

Do you explain natural animal behavior to people?

Seriously, does your best friend have four legs?

Do you have a similar story to tell? Then you have a passion for helping animals.

BURN OUT AND COMPASSION FATIGUE

Wildlife rehabilitation can be stressful, time-consuming, and emotionally taxing. Compassion fatigue is a term used in health care professions. It comes from being exposed to trauma that comes from others, in this case, injured or orphaned wildlife. It can often be an emotional roller coaster.

Before you even begin wildlife rehabilitation you need to understand the importance of priorities and making sure you take time for self-care.

Time management is an important business tool that will also benefit your personal life. Schedule in time for taking an herbal bath, reading to your children, or having a glass of wine with your significant other. Remember YOU are important!

WORK WITH A VET

It is very important to have a good working relationship with your veterinarian. Some states even require that your vet sign off on your paperwork in order to show medical commitment.

Finding a vet that will see wildlife can be tricky. Not all vets will see wildlife or exotic animals in their practice. Furthermore, while some vets will give a discount, vet care can easily be your highest expense.

Some medical procedures you can do yourself and your vet may be willing to give you some training to address common but minor conditions. However, such things as X-rays, setting a bone, repairing a severely crushed turtle shell, stitches, or performing an amputation requires a veterinarian.

VOLUNTEERS

Most rehabbers are volunteers. A few people may also be wildlife biologists and work for the state parks or the Department of Fish and Wildlife. Many wildlife rehabilitators have part or full-time jobs to support their passion and/or their families.

In addition, many rehabbers pay for their expenses out of their own pockets. You can ask for donations or do fundraisers as long as you are transparent.

You may decide to go through the process to become a non-profit which allows your donors to take a tax credit. It also lets you write grant applications, although there are not many grant opportunities for wildlife rescue compared to the rescue of domestic animals.

Wildlife rehabilitators do not have to have a college degree. They come from all different walks of life. What brings us together is compassion for animals and a desire to help them.

Volunteering for a licensed wildlife rehabilitator is a good way to find out if you want to become a rehabber. Many wildlife rehabilitators accept volunteers. Finding a mentor is a good idea.

More about having volunteers and interns as helpers in an upcoming chapter.

CAREERS In Wildlife Rehabilitation

Some people are wildlife rehabilitators as part of their job. Jobs such as wildlife biologists, environmental educators, zookeepers, or park rangers may include an aspect of wildlife rehabilitation. These jobs require a college degree in biology, environmental science, or something similar.

Having a wildlife rehabilitation license or experience may help you get a job and set you apart. Some veterinary techs specialize in exotic animals including wildlife.

Some people find work for larger non-profit wildlife sanctuaries or rehab centers that are able to offer paid positions.

Others may work for government or non-profits that assist during natural disasters such as oil spills, hurricanes, or wildfires.

PROFESSIONAL LICENSE OR PERMIT

Why bother to get a professional license or permit? I can take care of baby animals without it. Sadly, I hear this a lot.

There are many people who rehab wildlife illegally. Those people can receive fines or jail time if caught. However, the real tragedy is that in many areas the officers will often kill the animals and not try to place them with a licensed professional. I saw this happen several times in Kentucky.

Wildlife Rehabilitation is a profession. Just like Nursing or Teaching (which we do) we need to maintain certain standards. Having a license not only helps you comply with the law but also shows people you take your job seriously.

How Do I Get Licensed To Become A Wildlife Rehabilitator?

Each state has procedures you must follow to become a wildlife rehabilitator. These will be listed either under the state office for fish and wildlife or the state's department for natural resources. Common procedures are taking a test, course, or getting a number of volunteer hours under a licensed rehabilitator.

Many states require the rehabber to take the class The Basics in Wildlife Rehabilitation from IWRC plus classes for continuing education to become licensed. (see the Resources section)

This class is offered across the United States at various times. In addition, they offer it in several countries around the world. They are typically hosted by a college or local wildlife group. You just have to check the International Wildlife Rehabilitation Council website to see what locations are scheduled.

CERTIFIED WILDLIFE REHABILITATOR

The IWRC also offers a professional certificate that seeks to raise the minimum standard of knowledge and care for wildlife rehabilitation around the world.

This consists of taking an exam to show you have an advanced level of knowledge and professionalism.

You can learn more about this certificate on their website. They also give a list of topics you should be familiar with and examples.

FEDERAL LICENSES

In addition to getting a state license, there is also one federal license given through the USDA and one given through the USFW.

USDA APHIS

If you plan to have educational animals or do any type of outreach programs with animals, then you need to obtain a USDA Class C license. This regulates cage size and care for wildlife on display or used in community outreach.

BIRD LICENSE

The Basics class is for those that want to be licensed in mammals, reptiles, and/or birds. However, to receive a bird license you must go above and beyond the Basics class in all states.

Migratory birds fall under the licensing of the US Dept of Fish and Wildlife and have further requirements. This would include raptors and songbirds.

The Business End

WHY IS THIS IMPORTANT FOR REHABILITATORS?

Wildlife rehabilitators are devoted loving people. I know this because I am one and I hang around with like-minded friends! That devotion sometimes leads us to make poor decisions.

Do you know how to say "NO"? I'm working on that one too.

Rehabbers need to view themselves as a business. The business (your rehab center) must take in funds to support the growth of your product (your babies). If you take in products faster than you take in money your business will be in debt. Often this means personal debt.

This is a frequent problem. We have a hard time setting limits. However, when we do not set limits, we often stress ourselves financially as well as emotionally. I have definitely been there!

I feel that this is the main reason people stop rehabbing.

Treating your center as a business is very important. This is where all that record-keeping is essential. Keep track of how much you spend on formula, how much your babies eat, and what foods you are buying at the store.

YOU ARE A BUSINESS!

I cannot tell you how many rehabbers I talk to personally or see on Facebook that does not consider themselves as a small business.

*** Look in the mirror and repeat after me: I am a business and a professional.

When you view yourself as a business and a professional it will help you to have the respect and admiration you so rightly deserve. (Sing the Aretha Franklin song in your head now).

TRACKING YOUR COSTS

This chapter leads into many other topics – running a business, finding donors, writing grants, and fundraising. All-important topics. There is very little quality information geared towards rehabbers on these topics.

Tracking your costs is very important. Don't just automatically reach for your personal credit card.

Set up a bank account for your business so you have a record of expenses. If you personally place money in that account, make a note to yourself because you can count that as a donation.

Talk to an accountant. Ask your followers if anyone is a CPA or financial planner and is willing to donate some time to educate you or help with taxes.

One of the advantages of being a non-profit is the ability to write grants. Grants are sums of monies given to a non-profit to accomplish a task. You may get a grant to build an enclosure or one to educate the public.

Grant writing is competitive as there is much less money available than there is a need. For those of us doing wildlife rescue, opportunities are fewer because many pet grants will exclude wildlife rescues from applications.

However, you can extend your grant outreach to include education and outreach programs. This gain helps your overall outreach program and connect with donors.

HOW TO GET SUPPLIES DONATED

It's easy to make a list but the next part is getting the actual products. Obviously, you can go to the store and buy all the things you need. However, costs do add up fast and you may not have enough money in your budget. Here are some ideas to get you started.

1. Make an Amazon Wishlist - anyone can make a public Wishlist and then share it to social media and/or in an email newsletter. Many people use Amazon and it's easy and convenient for them to just add something from your list to their cart. Then Amazon ships that item to you.

2. Chris's Squirrels and More also does a Wishlist and makes it so you can share it on social media. Personally, I love her store, but I find it hard to convince my followers to shop there as it's not familiar to them. Since they are frequently on Amazon it's more familiar.

3. Donations from social media followers- tell people what you need, post needs on your social media, and see what you receive. Local people are often quite willing to bring in old towels or purchase things they can pick up easily like paper towels or dog food.

4. Donations from corporations or companies. You can also ask for donations from businesses. I will be honest and tell you that

most businesses will want you to be a non-profit. However, places in your community such as where you shop, your church, kids school, or library may have a bulletin board you can put a flyer on.

5. Your local doctor or vet's office may be willing to give you expired products. Things such as syringes, latex gloves, and wormer all have expiration dates. A doctor or veterinarian can't use them after expiration, but you can because your work on wildlife is typically "off label".

6. The internet has become the way we find out information. Having a website for your rehabilitation center is crucial for your success. A website lets you tell people what you do, how and when to contact you, educate the public, gain supporters, and raise money.

My Side Gig Came from My Website!

I actually ended up with a side gig because I started a small website on SquareSpace back in 2015 for Fox Run EEC. I began writing an informative blog and playing around with Canva for graphic design. My website was getting 5000 persons coming to it from all around the country. Next thing I knew I was taking courses in how to become a content creator. (Currently Fox Run averages about 30,000 a month in traffic)

Then POOF! I was writing and managing social media for other animal related businesses. As of this writing I currently work with 6 other businesses in some capacity whether designing websites, writing blogs, or doing their social media. You can contact me at foxrunwritingservices@yahoo.com to learn more about that service.

Social Media

Social Media is a great tool. If you are like me, you may get sucked down many rabbit holes with the buns! Use social media– BUT DON'T LET IT USE YOU. I have seriously reduced my personal time on social media and just view it as a work tool.

Have a plan for posting educational content or updates about how the babies are doing. Plan specific times to post updates about your intakes. People do love to see pictures of your intakes.

I make educational posts like this one that I put on Facebook, Twitter, and YouTube.

WHY YOU NEED A WEBSITE

As we all know, websites are an important way for businesses to talk about their products and educate the population on what they do. People today feel very comfortable going online to seek out information.

However, many of you think that only "big" for-profit companies need websites. Maybe you are a home-based rehab center, and you don't feel like a business at all. Both are mistakes.

HELP PEOPLE FIND YOU

A website is often your first line of communication with a finder. When someone comes across a wildlife emergency, they typically just press the mic button on their cell phone and say, "Wildlife rehabilitator near me". A good website puts you at the top of the list.

In addition to this having a Google business page is a wonderful way to get noticed.

Do keep in mind that you may want to use a PO Box for your official address. I had issues with people showing up unannounced or throwing baby animals over the fence in the middle of the night. In addition, people would call me telling me they were at the post office!

CREDIBILITY

Your website allows people to get to know you and gives you credibility as a real business. It's a terrible fact of life that wildlife rehabbers are not given the respect they deserve. Your website will promote you as a legitimate business.

It also shows your audience that you are doing "real work". Cute pictures of baby animals doesn't hurt!

FAQ'S

FAQs are Frequently Asked Questions. As a wildlife rehabber, you don't always have time to answer the phone. **Yes, it rings non-stop**. I know!! Even if you have an intern or dedicated administrative assistant on your team the phone is a constant source of interruption.

Having basic information on your website can help reduce phone calls. Things such as where you are located and what species you take are common questions. If you are full your website can link to your state listing or the national Animal Help Now APP to help the finder locate someone else.

In addition, your voice mail message can direct people to your website for more information.

Collect Donations

You can collect donations and do campaigns on social media which are important sources of revenue. However, it often takes the platforms 6 – 8 weeks to cut you a check. The advantage of having a website and linking it to PayPal or Stripe is you have money almost immediately.

Also, a website is under your control, and this is important. Social media algorithms do not always mesh with your marketing plan. In simple terms, Facebook, Instagram, and Twitter all decide who and when people see your posts. A website allows you to put it out there on your terms.

GIVE MORE IN DEPTH INFORMATION

A website is also a fantastic way to continue the education process. Your website allows you to go into detail on a problem or what to do factor.

For instance, on my Facebook page, I often put memes or little bite-sized bits of information on wildlife. You know – the meme that shows the fawn curled up in the woods because that's what it's supposed to do or the one where it says put the bunny back several times.

Your website can continue to carry on that conversation. My website has a blog that has steps to determine if a baby is truly an orphan and what to do. I also have an active wildlife blog that gets readers from around the world that gives in detail information on a species.

I continue that via the YouTube channel. While my YouTube channel also includes gardening and homesteading videos, I post wildlife education and wildlife rehabilitation videos as well. You can put your videos on your website.

STEPS TO STARTING A WEBSITE

Choose a domain name and register it. This will often be your business name. Just do a simple web check first to see if anyone already owns the name you wish to use. Then you can go on Google, Square Space, or GoDaddy to find out if the name is available. I am on Square Space, so I just do everything through them.

I have an extremely long domain name! It is recommended that you keep your name down to 15 characters so that's it's easy to remember and find.

Choose a host or a website provider. There are several out there with a variety of plans and options. You can always pick a smaller personal plan and build up to a business site with more commercial options. I started with a lower cost personal site on Square Space and paid for one year because that was a cheaper option than paying month to month. Since then, I have upgraded to the business plan but you can do the basics with a personal plan.

COSTS?

I have two thoughts for you if you are digging in your heals over the cost of a website.

The first is the age-old expression – You have to spend money to make money. Look at your website as a tool to help you grow your business and bring in more money. Your website will pay for itself by bringing in revenue from donations, affiliate links, and a store.

The second is that a website is going to help you do your job well. Your website can do many tasks such as having intake forms, reducing repetitive conversation, and showcasing your events or activities. You don't have to hand out printed material, just direct them to the website.

In addition, your website helps to carry out your mission. As a non-profit one of my missions is to educate the public.

Can you get a free website? Yes. Are they worth it? No!

Free websites are hard to edit and update and are typically covered in spammy ads that you have no control over. They look terrible and are hard to navigate. You can lose business with a cheap, unappealing website.

There are several good websites including SquareSpace and Wix that are easy to get going. These are often considered plug and play websites because they don't need a knowledge of coding to get started. Just some basic creativity and a willingness to learn some graphic design and visual presentation.

For Profit or Non-Profit

Wildlife Rehabilitation is a business. You can make that business either a for-profit or a non-profit. There are advantages and disadvantages to both ways.

As a licensed wildlife rehabilitator, you offer a service. You are not only helping the animals, but you also help the community and are a supportive team member with other agencies such as Fish and Wildlife, Animal Control, and the Department of Natural Resources. This applies if you are a small mom and pop shop or a large center.

There are a lot of misunderstandings when it comes to animal rescue services. Some assume you have to be a non-profit (you don't). Some think non-profits can't make money (they can) and some say that as a for-profit you can't accept any charity (you can).

FOR-PROFIT

- A business that offers a service or a product
- Often makes money through investments and sales
- Leadership is typically the owner or a partnership
- Often do not qualify for grants
- Business taxes apply
- Easy application process depending on the type of business

The title for-profit businesses make it sound like for-profits are rolling in the money. They are not always making a profit. In fact, many lose money each year.

Many wildlife rehabilitation centers who are technically a for-profit business do not even set themselves up as a business. This is a big mistake. Not only can you get in trouble with your state you are missing out on some tax benefits.

Take the time (and sometimes a small fee) to set yourself up as a DBA (doing business as), sole proprietorship, partnership or an LLC. Depending on your set up you may be able to deduct or appreciate business expenses, which will help you with your taxes.

NON-PROFIT

- A business that promotes a social cause
- Makes money through donations, sponsorships, and sales
- Leadership is the director and the Board of Directors
- May write grants for funds and take corporation and private donations
- Tax exemptions and donors can get tax benefits
- Must fill out forms and apply with the state and federal government

One of the biggest misconceptions about non-profit businesses is that they can't make money. Non-profits, just like any other business have expenses. They need to have an income in order to pay those expenses.

One of the biggest "issues" with starting a non-profit is the complexity of the paperwork. Formal paperwork needs to be submitted that states your mission, names of board members, and what types of activities you plan to conduct.

BUSINESS RESOURCES

There are a lot of good resources to help you start and manage a small business.

The Small Business Administration provides free one on one counseling and classes to help you get started or resolve business issues. They have district offices all over the USA.

Many Universities have business development centers.

WHAT IS A GRANT?

Government, community organizations, and companies give out money to help support non-profits that are serving community need. They often reflect the company's products or goals. For instance, many pet corporations give grants to animal rescuers. As an animal rescuer, you are doing a valuable service.

Grants are different from crowdfunding. Crowdfunding is when you ask individuals to support you by raising money for a specific goal. The Baby Warm incubators are a good example of crowdfunding.

A grant does not have to be paid back. Typically, you make a final report and show how the money was used. For example, if you received money for materials to build an enclosure, you would show the receipts and a photo of the final project.

HOW DO I GET A GRANT?

To receive a grant, you must apply for a specific (the people giving away the money). The applications are a serious undertaking as they can be quite lengthy.

DO I HAVE TO BE A NON-PROFIT TO QUALIFY FOR A GRANT?

Not always however, about 90% of grants are awarded to non-profits, schools, and other government entities. Part of the grant application shows you are spending money in a responsible way. Occasionally, grants ask about financial records.

There is one group of scholarships in wildlife rehabilitation that is open to all rehabbers. They are offered through the National Wildlife Rehabilitation Association. NWRA has scholarships for training and one for wildlife housing.

HAVING A PLAN

Grant writing is time-consuming. There is a long process of finding and writing the grant. Grants have open and close dates for when they are taking applications.

In addition, grant applications become available at various times of the year. So, you need to have an organized system so you can track and be ready to fill out your application. Make notes in your calendar to plan for upcoming applications.

Many grants follow a similar pattern. One way that people save time is to pre-write sections that are similar such as describing their mission and what they do.

It's worth noting that you may spend a lot of time on a grant that's worth only $300. The larger the organization the larger the grant they may receive. In addition, grant writing is kind of like a credit score. If you get a grant of $300 and make up a nice final presentation, then word will get around and you will be able to get a bigger grant next time.

Another option is to seek out a professional grant writer and see if they do pro bono work for fledgling operations. You may find someone who will volunteer some time to write a grant for you.

Pick and choose the grants you submit. Federal grants are notorious for their complexity. However, smaller foundations may have a shorter application because they like you are strapped for time and resources. Remember each grant application gets read by several people at the foundation before they get together and discuss them.

Working With Volunteers and Interns

You don't have to be a non-profit to invite volunteers or interns into your facility.

Volunteers are people that come and offer their help because they are passionate about animal rescue and believe in what you are doing. Volunteers donate their time and skills to help with wildlife care, paperwork, or education programs.

Interns are people that want to learn a skill and need hands-on experiences. Typically, they are college students. Foremost interns want (need) to have educational experiences. They may be getting college credit for their experiences and need to do a project or paper at the end of the term. You may need to fill out a form on the student's attendance and participation.

For both volunteers and interns you will want to have some basic expectations and rules in place. Having a training program and a written set of guidelines is important. Volunteers need clear and concise instructions. Interns need guidance.

PROS

- Free or inexpensive labor
- Share your knowledge
- You will learn new things
- Build community connections

CONS

- Can be hard to find good candidates

- Insurance and legalities depending on your state
- Interns need training and supervision

Volunteers typically come from your community and drive to your home/center each week at a designated time. For the sake of planning, you may want to ask them to have a consistent schedule.

Interns may come from your community or from halfway across the country! You may choose to provide benefits such as housing and food.

Interns coming out of college classes may have learned about new techniques or read interesting studies. Keep your mind open and you may pick up some tricks of the trade.

I would say the biggest disadvantage of good interns is finding them. Finding candidates can be challenging and depends on many factors such as your location, any stipend, on-site housing etc. The IWRC (see Resources) has a job board for internships and jobs on their website. Members may post a listing. I also worked with local universities to find candidates.

One disadvantage is that you may need to expand your insurance plan and/or adapt to comply with state laws. I carry liability insurance but require interns to have their own health insurance.

WAGE LAWS

Wage laws vary from state to state. In general, for interns, you must pay minimum wage unless you offer an educational component for the person's work. The government wants an internship to benefit the intern and provide an educational component.

This is something that varies with states, and you will want to check with your attorney about.

STIPEND

A stipend is monies paid to help offset costs. Typically used for interns it does not have to meet minimum wage. A stipend does not depend on the number of hours the intern works and is not performance-based.

For instance, you might offer a stipend of $50 per week for 20 hours of work.

Keep in mind that although your intern may be receiving food and housing, they may have other expenses such as car insurance and gas.

Kidnapping

Kidnapping is an unfortunate event when humans steal baby wild animals from their natural homes. Sometimes people kidnap wildlife because they think they are helping or rescuing the baby. Often humans kidnap wildlife because they want an exotic pet.

Taking a wild animal from its home for any reason is kidnapping. If you feel the baby is genuinely orphaned or you can see injuries, then contact a wildlife rehabilitator to get their advice.

There are many normal reasons that wildlife babies are left alone.

WILD ANIMAL PETS

But It's So Cute – I Want to Take Care Of It – It Will Make A Great Pet

NO NO NO AND NO – do you hear these sentiments often?

Here is what I have said.

First please think of the animal. It deserves to lead a natural life. Not a life in a cage as a show toy. It deserves to be respected. Leave it in the wild. If you are not willing to transport it to a licensed rehabber, then walk away and let nature take its course.

A frightened hurt animal is not a photo op. Use your cell phone to call a rehabber or the conservation officer. Don't subject the animal to a selfie with you. This often leads to death from stress.

WILD ANIMALS MAKE BAD PETS

Wildlife rehabilitators get lots of calls from people who have kept wildlife as pets and are now having behavior issues (I know about this personally!).

Take raccoons for example. They are very cute, smart, and amusing as kits. But guess what? HORMONES!

When raccoons reach puberty they turn into typical teenagers, only worse. They bite, they poop everywhere, and they become very destructive. If they are living in the house, it's a bad scene.

What often happens is that their "family" suddenly hates them because they have been "bad" and kicks them out of the house. That raccoon has no idea how to survive.

No one has taught him to fish for food or climb trees to get to safety. These are things a mother raccoon does – or a trained rehabber. That pet will soon die of starvation or become a neighborhood menace and become victims of human abuse and get shot. It's not worth it!

WHY IS THAT WILD ANIMAL BABY ALONE?

There are many normal reasons that a baby animal may be alone.

- Deer leave their babies because the fawn has no odor and they do this for protection
- Juveniles, such as foxes and groundhogs, are often just exploring the outdoors as a natural part of maturing.

- Cottontails are weaned at 4 weeks (the size of a tennis ball) and look like babies.
- Parents may just have left the baby to look for food.
- Mom could have been scared by humans and is watching and waiting for them to leave
- Squirrels and baby birds fall out of the nest

THINK ABOUT THESE QUESTIONS

Wildlife rehabilitators often ask leading questions so that they can ascertain whether there is a need for rehabilitation or can we reunite the baby with its mother.

Ask these questions when the finders call you.

1. Tell me how you found the baby

2. Describe what the baby was doing when you found them

3. Do you hear or see a mother nearby

4. Does the baby have visual injuries or appear to be unhealthy (emaciated, lice).

FINDERS CALLS TO WILDLIFE REHABBERS OFTEN ARE VERY EMOTIONAL

Fawns are a great example of kidnap victims. They are cute and alone and everyone assumes the worst. I get these calls a lot –

Finder - Hi I found an orphaned baby deer and I don't know what to do. Please help me!

Rehabber – Yes, ma'am. Can you tell me how you found the baby?

Finder – well I was taking a walk with Trixie, that's my little dog, and we came across this poor baby all by herself. She looks like she's starving to death and is just crying and making this sad noise.

Rehabber – ma'am where is the fawn now?

Finder – well she was so distraught that I took her to the house, put her on the couch and tucked her in. Trixie is keeping her company.

Rehabber – can you text me a picture of the fawn, please. I need a picture to see if the fawn looks healthy.

(At this point I am rolling my eyes and making faces at my phone)

When the picture comes in of a nice healthy fawn, I then explain to the caller that deer leave their babies on purpose. I give them a quick lesson on deer parenting and how this is still a very loved baby. I tell the finder to take the fawn back to where they found it (without their dog in tow) and PUT THE BABY BACK!

Sometimes people will argue this point and refuse or make excuses. As a wildlife rehabilitator, I do explain the law at this point and why we have wildlife laws. If they flat out refuse, I say in a nice non-aggressive way – Ma'am if you would like me to send an officer to your house to help you, I will do that.

At that point, I end the call, say a quick prayer for the fawn, and try to remember what I was doing! Depending on your state the rehabber may need to document the call.

Some wildlife rehabbers do try to follow through and make sure the fawn gets back. That is a personal decision based on your time, energy, and goals.

Stealing Baby Animals to Make Money

There is an element of the population that will deliberately steal wildlife to sell them for money.

The following kidnapping story is one where I became involved.

TRUE STORY

Several years ago in May, I had driven to Danville, Kentucky to pick up my son who was a student at Centre College. My phone rang and I answered the call to one of my local Kentucky Fish and Wildlife Officers. He asked me if I had room for another fawn. Yes, I said, however, I was in Danville picking up Caleb and it would be three hours before I arrived home.

"That's OK he said, I have to hunt down the guy – this is a kidnap victim".

Let me just pause for a moment to tell you a kidnap victim is the term rehabbers use to describe an animal that is deliberately or inadvertently taken from its family when the baby is perfectly fine.

Officer Chris went on to say that someone had taken a baby deer from the woods and was SELLING it via Facebook in a yard sale. Just let me say OMG!

God love KYFW that day. They chased that fawn over several counties, gave out citations, and finally ended up at my house at 11 pm at night. With two fawns no less.

And one more for the road – pun intended. The picture above is of Harley the fawn in this next story. From a post I made on Facebook.

This is a perfect example of why we need to leave fawns alone. This beautiful, healthy little guy was kidnapped yesterday. The story goes that he was "found" sleeping on the side of the road. He was picked up by a man on a motorcycle and ridden to a railroad station and left there. They called KYFW. Officer Ping tried to find out where the fawn came from but sadly could not. So, he was brought to Fox Run. And while we love all our wildlife, we are very sad because we can never be as good a parent as his biological mom!

WHEN DO WILDLIFE BABIES NEED INTERVENTION?

As a rehabber, it is your job to know when that baby animal needs intervention. Remember that intervention does not necessarily mean you cannot attempt to reunite the family. In some cases, some short-term medical intervention may be necessary, but you are still within a window of opportunity.

Cases where a quick fix will support health and you can attempt a reunion.

- Slight dehydration of less than 5%
- Parasites – not a heavy load
- Abrasions, scraps, shallow wounds where washing and applying ointment will help
- Turtles with minimal cracked shells (shell not hanging or exposing muscle or organs)
- A slight concussion from being hit by a car or bird window strike that needs monitoring for a few hours

Cases where the baby will need more long-term intervention.

- Dehydration of over 5 %

- Heavy parasite load that interferes with their health and causing dehydration, anemia, diarrhea.
- Serious wounds where the animal is bleeding, has exposed bone or organs, or maggots.
- Possible serious concussion – the animal has been hit by car or baby has fallen on a hard surface.
- Breathing problems
- In shock or unconscious
- Cold, low body temp, shivering
- Parent is deceased – hit by a car or trapped and killed
- Emaciated or starving
- Reuniting failed

WORKING WITH YOUR LOCAL HUMANE SOCIETY AND POLICE DEPARTMENTS

Working with your local animal control, local, and state police is very important. These are the people who are out on the front lines and often get the first call. It is important for them to know how to respond effectively.

Wildlife is often a grey area. Education is very important.

I have offered free training to my animal control officers and police/sheriff departments. I have a PowerPoint I made that goes over some basic wildlife parenting, how to determine if the baby is truly orphaned and steps to take.

Don't assume they have had training in wildlife concerns. Most animal control agencies don't give training in handling wildlife. This is a good way to get to know those departments and form collaboration opportunities.

This is also a good time to state your transportation policies. In Kentucky I covered a very large 7 county area. I didn't have the time or money to travel and pick up babies. I let agencies know that upfront. Be direct. They are paid with taxpayer dollars to do their jobs. They often don't realize that you are a volunteer.

WORKING WITH PET SURRENDERS AND PET CONFISCATIONS

Wildlife rehabilitators often get calls on pet surrenders and pet confiscations. A pet surrender is when a kidnap victim has been kept as a pet for a period of time. This may be months or years. Eventually the animal "wilds up" and becomes difficult to handle.

Or that person has been "caught" by a Fish and Wildlife officer and the animal was confiscated. With luck, the FW officer may have given the person time to place the animal with a licensed rehabber. Your officer may show up at your door or you will get a hysterical call from the person with the warning.

Sadly, however, sometimes the confiscated pet is euthanized by the officer.

As a wildlife rehabilitator, having a plan for these situations is very important. Your plan may be simply that you do not take pet surrenders. Your plan may be that you accept them depending on age and how likely they will be to rehabilitate.

Pet surrenders have their own set of issues and problems. For one, they are teenage or adult animals. Sadly, they are often very very confused and stressed. They are dependent on humans for food, shelter, and a sense of safety. But at the same time, their bodies are telling them "hunt", "have sex" or "defend yourself".

Many surrenders are raccoons which along with fawns are the most common kidnap victims. As we all know raccoons are very cute and fun when they are little. But hormones kick in and watch out!

In the past, I have taken in one or two raccoon pet surrenders each year. I charged the owner for that service because they are the ones responsible, and it takes money and time to rehabilitate.

I have had the KYFW tell me that you can't rehabilitate an adult raccoon. I strongly disagree. I have had success in reintroducing pet raccoons to the wild. It is a long process and requires a lot of interventions, but the animal's instincts do kick in. They just need to be supported along the way.

Below is Boomer. He was two when he came and just needed time. He started out in an enclosure, moved up to free range in the barn yard, and eventually started venturing into the woods. We gave him emotional and nutritional support till he was ready.

Transportation

For those of you with a passion to help wildlife but are not ready to commit to being a rehabber. One simple way is to put a wildlife rescue kit in your car. In fact, all licensed rehabilitators should have a wildlife kit in the car.

The things in this kit will help you to safely catch and move a wild animal so that you can transport them to a licensed wildlife rehabilitator.

While it is illegal for you to keep wildlife without a license, most states have Good Samaritan laws that allow you to pick up and transport to a licensed facility.

I have a YouTube Video on How To Make a Wildlife Rescue Car Kit

YOUR SAFETY IS IMPORTANT

Always make sure that you pull over in a safe spot and consider traffic when checking on the animal. Put on your emergency blinkers.

Having a Fluro-vest that can be easily seen by oncoming traffic will keep you visible. Your kit should also include a strong flashlight and extra batteries.

What To Have In Your Car

LEATHER GLOVES

Welding gloves are a must. Animals who are hurt and afraid can and do bite. Welding gloves are made of thick leather and will protect your hands and lower arms.

GOGGLES

Protect your eyes. This is especially important if you are picking up a bird as they may try to peck at your face.

LATEX GLOVES

Always wear latex/vinyl gloves when you pick up an animal or inspect a wound. Orphaned babies especially are typically covered with lice or fleas. In addition, if the animal has open wounds, you don't want the blood to touch your bare skin.

CLEANER

Baby wipes and hand sanitizer are both great to have for cleanup after handling the animal.

Simple hand warmers are great to start to slowly warm up baby in the car

HAND WARMERS

These chemical active hand warmers are great for an emergency. You only need to shake to activate. Eyes closed, babies cannot produce their own heat and hyperthermia is a real danger to their life.

Never place heat directly on or under the baby. This may cause overheating and they may not be able to escape. Wrap the hand warmer in a small cloth and place it next to, but not on the baby.

CUTTERS

Scissors or wire cutters. Don't go cutting a fence on private land without permission. Obviously, that would be breaking the law.

However, it's good to have a pair of wire cutters in case you find an animal entangled in a fence.

Sometimes you find a turtle or a bird whose legs are wrapped with fishing line. They may simply need to be cut free.

IMPORTANT NUMBERS

Look up the numbers for wildlife rehabilitation facilities in your area. Make a note if they take certain species. Not all rehabbers take all animals.

Download the Animal Help Now App on your phone. This app works throughout the USA and can help you locate wildlife rehabilitators. You simply enter your location, and it will give you any licensed rehabilitators in your area.

TRY TO MOVE THEM WITHOUT PICKING THEM UP

Use a cat carrier or cardboard box. It's important to have a safe and secure way to transport the animal. If they are loose, they can panic and cause further injuries to themselves.

If you can, move your carrier right in front of their body. Use the square of cardboard to gently lift and move them into the cage.

Help them feel safe and secure. Towels are a great tool in picking up an animal. Throw the towel over them and quickly pick them up and place them in the carrier.

After you have them in a cage or box use another towel to place over the cage. The dark will make them feel safer.

Pillowcases work well for picking up small animals. Use a rubber band to secure the open end.

You Need to Emphasis with Finders!

Never hold a wild animal on your lap or in your arms. An animal that appears calm and cuddly is most likely in shock. In addition, it may wake up and panic at an inopportune moment.

Don't let children handle or play with the baby. This is NOT the time for a selfie! This is a personal pet peeve of mine. I have had people send me cutsie pics and then text me 30 minutes later because the cute baby was dead. Well yea.

Animals can have a heart attack and die from stress. Unfortunately, they are programmed to feel stress from our voices and smell. So, limit handling and noise.

I literally had a young woman come into the center carrying a full-grown groundhog like a baby and singing it a lullaby. The groundhog had an obvious concussion. I explained to the woman that this was unsafe for her, and the groundhog and she became totally unhinged. So fortunate that I had a volunteer with me who was from a military family. I was able to get the ground hog and place it safely in a cage and the volunteer was able to corral the woman back to her car. We assured her we would keep her posted on her baby's health. Yikes. The next day the ground hog felt much better and was mad as hell!

HOW TO TELL IF A WILD BABY ANIMAL NEEDS INTERVENTION?

Most wildlife rehabilitators deal with injured and orphaned babies. We never want to create an orphan. Wild mom is the best possible mother for the baby.

Call your local rehabilitator for advice or any questions.

If you see baby mammals on the side of the road look around and see if you see mom's body. A dead mom tells you these babies are orphans and need intervention.

Other signs that babies may be orphans are:

- Covered in parasites such as fleas, ticks, and/or lice
- Matted or dirty fur
- Crying and moving in a circular manner
- Obvious dehydration or emaciation

OPOSSUMS

Opossums are a unique situation. First, sadly they are often hit on the road. Second, female possums have a pouch that may contain living babies.

You can check the pouch. This is definitely a case for wearing latex gloves. Possums are scavengers.

An adult male opossum has pronounced testicles so you can check for sex first. Also remember, possums can and do "play possum". Use care because you may have an animal that is just injured.

The pouch does not open at the time of death so you will need to locate the flap and pull it open to check. Sometimes you don't have to open it because you can see the babies moving around in there.

TURTLES

You may also encounter a turtle that has been hit on the road and has a broken shell. Shells can be glued back together, and the turtle can most likely be re-released.

Always make sure you note the location where you found the turtle. Turtles have a homing sense and must be released back into their territory.

Using your latex gloves pick up the turtle gently and place them in your carrier. Turtles do feel pain. Don't push on the shell pieces.

Never use any kind of tape on a turtle shell. This can push the shell into delicate organs and can also cause more damage when it is removed. I can't tell you how many people brought me turtles wrapped in duct tape.

Not all rehabbers take reptiles so make sure you locate one who does and add them to your list.

SUPPLIES

Every winter I clean out my wildlife rehabilitation medicine cabinet. I take inventory of what I have and what I will need for the coming year. You can easily stock up on supplies and equipment to meet your center's needs.

This chapter will help you know what to buy to stock up on medical and first aid supplies for your wildlife rehab.

WHERE DO I BUY MEDICAL SUPPLIES?

You will gather your medical supplies from a variety of places. I order many of my supplies online with Amazon. Supplies can come from your local drug store or Walmart.

- Veterinarian/Farm supply companies such as Tractor Supply and Jeffers Pet Supplies carry many over-the-counter animal medicines and first aid supplies.
- Specialty stores such as <u>Chris's Squirrels and More</u> and <u>Henry's Pets</u> offer products for rehabbers.
- Prescription items such as Lactated Ringers Fluids will need to come from your vet.

YOUR MEDICINE CABINET

You need to have a dedicated area to store supplies. This may be shelves, a closet, or kitchen style cabinets. I recommend that your storage place has doors and the ability to be locked.

I use an old food heating unit that came from a hospital kitchen remodel. It meets all my criteria and has shelves that can be pulled out or moved around. The only thing I don't like about it is that it is quite deep, and I tend to lose things in the back.

Organize and label your supplies. Trust me, when that baby comes in that is severely dehydrated or a turtle with a very broken shell, you will want to be able to move fast and know where everything is located. I use plastic totes inside my cabinet to store like items and keep things clean.

LISTS OF SUPPLIES

I will list things in stages - from common inexpensive things to those you may need to work up to.

COMMON HOUSEHOLD ITEMS

These are things you probably have around your house and even in your own medicine cabinet. They cost under $10.00 new

To get you started you can also buy a pet first aid kit.

- Tweezers
- Bandage scissors
- Q-Tips
- Alcohol
- Hydrogen Peroxide
- Witch Hazel (or grow your own)
- Iodine
- Saline eye solution

- Eyedropper
- Antibiotic cream, antifungal agent, and anticoccidial
- Matches for burning ticks or you can stick them in alcohol
- Bandages of various sizes such as vet wrap, gauze wraps, and squares, bandage tape
- You will need a variety of gauze pads in various sizes
- Adhesive tape
- Disposable gloves
- Rectal pet thermometer (several for various species)

These are items you will want but are a little bit pricier. They cost between $10.00 and $50.00 new.

- Stethoscope
- Hair clippers with #40 blades (used to clip hair away from a wound). You don't need a fancy set just something simple.
- Gram Scale - A gram scale is used to weigh a smaller baby on intake. Grams (from the metric system) are what are used most widely to determine fluids, meds, and formula amounts. I like this one that has a dish on top so babies don't fall off.
- For fawns or larger babies, I just use a human scale and weigh just me and then me holding the baby. Then subtract.
- Standard scales in ounces can also be used and then you can easily do the conversion on Google. I have a very nice farmer's market scale that I use to weigh babies on.
- Syringes and Needles - these should be on your priority list since they are both very important. You will use syringes for feeding as well as delivering fluids and medicines. Common needle sizes to have on hand are 25, 22, 20. You will need a variety of needles in different sizes. It seems backward but the smaller the number the bigger the needle.

- Wormer - you will need several different kinds for different species of wildlife and different species of worms. A good all-around one that's not too expensive is pyrantel pamoate.
- Don't buy the cheap wormers at your local bargain store. During tests, these often end up being of poor quality with little

acting drugs. You will go through a lot of wormers so invest in the good stuff
- Capstar (non-prescription) It works well on fleas and also kills maggots.
- Chlorhexidine is a bacterial disinfectant. Great for cleaning wounds. I also use it to soak turtles who have been hit by cars.
- Heating pads - part of your medical care will be to get the animal warm. Often their body temperature has dropped due to not having a mom, shock, or illness. Getting them warm will be a priority. Heating pads often have an automatic shut-off. This is to protect humans. You don't want automatic shut off! You need constant heat. Look for a good quality heating pad made for pets as they don't usually have auto shut off and do have stronger cords.

THINGS TO SAVE FOR OR TO HAVE DONATED

These things are nice if you have them but can be more expensive and cost over $50.00 new.

Incubator - having an incubator to keep babies warm can be a real blessing. They surround the animal with consistent heat and are more thorough than a heating mat. The better ones have digital displays and settings, alarms, and a fan to circulate air. Brinsea makes small ones that are used in the pet industry that run in the $400-$800 range.

Baby Warm is a crowdfunding site that helps rehabbers get an incubator. It's not a donation! You are required to help raise the funds on your social media and website platforms. They assist by putting your information on their website.

At the time of publication, they use the [Brinsea TLC 40 Incubator](#) which retails on Amazon for $749.00.

Brinsea asks you to post a happy picture when you get yours – so here was mine!

Triage

As a rehabber you know that those first few hours, even minutes, are critical when a baby comes into your care. This care begins with your initial conversation with the finder. You will give instructions to the finder on what to do and begin a plan of action.

The steps that you take are important in order to give the best chances for survival or decide that humane euthanasia is the best option. For you the licensed wildlife rehabilitator this means that you will provide care in an efficient manner.

A baby who has been hit by a car and is bleeding profusely needs immediate care to stop the loss of blood. A baby who is orphaned, slightly dehydrated, and very frightened actually does best if placed in a warm dark quiet location prior to an exam.

Prioritize.

1. Initial location, capture, and translocation
2. Examination and assessment for rehabilitation
3. First aid and stabilization
4. Treatment
5. Recuperation and rehabilitation
6. Release (Best and Mullineaux 2003):

Elizabeth Mullineaux, a British Veterinarian, is one of the co-authors of BSAVA Manual of Wildlife Casualties. This is a great resource for a larger center or vets who work with wildlife cases.

ADMISSION OF THE BABY ANIMAL

Admitting a wild animal into your care requires some documentation and some paperwork. How in-depth this is may be decided by your state's requirements or the federal government requirements.

You may choose to use a written form that the finder fills out on arrival. You can also use an online form and have them fill it out before you admit the baby.

Don't stand around and chat. I often met people at the gate and handed them the clip board. I also gave them a card with website,

YouTube and Facebook information. This way I could extract myself and go tend the baby.

National Wildlife Rehabilitators Association and International Wildlife Rehabilitation Council put together the handbook MINIMUM STANDARDS FOR WILDLIFE REHABILITATION. The appendix section has several good examples of admitting forms. You can download this handbook for free.

WHAT TO ASK ON YOUR AMISSION FORM

- Name, address, phone number, and email of the finder.
- Species and numbers?
- Is the animal injured?
- Has the baby been given anything to eat and/or drink?
- Has the animal bitten or scratched anyone?
- Did the finder wear gloves?
- When and where was it found?

WHAT IS TRIAGE

Triage was first used on battlefields during times of war. Triage separates the critical emergencies from those that are less urgent.

On admittance, you will do a brief exam to confirm the species and the condition. This should be under 2two minutes. You can expect the animal to be stressed and in shock. This is especially true if the finder has been carrying it around and cuddling it.

Decide what treatments should come first. In their book, Wild Mammal Babies: the first 48 hours and beyond, Irene Ruth and Deb Gode have a wonderful exam and evaluation chart. In my first two years, I copied that chart and had it hanging up where I did triage.

BE PREPARED

You should know the animals' story - their medical history as brief as that may be. This will clue you in on what you may need to make your initial exam as brief and stress-free as possible.

One thing I often do is prepare while the finder is en-route. This actually helps me stay calm and get ready. Are they bringing an animal with an open wound? I will get out bandages, chlorhexidine ect.

My scale and stethoscope are always on the counter.

QUESTIONS TO ASK YOURSELF DURING THE INITIAL EXAM.

In The Box Exam

The first thing we are going to do is an in the box exam. Don't just quickly remove the animal. Take a moment to observe how the animal is acting before you go to pick it up.

This exam lets us see if the animal is lying or sitting normally. Check to see if the head is being held normally. In birds look at how they hold their wings. These are things you can't see as well once you pick that animal up.

If this animal presents itself with severe injuries or disease, there is no reason to remove it from the box and cause further stress. That animal may be a candidate for humane euthanasia.

BRIEF OUT OF BOX EXAM

This is a brief two-minute exam so to minimize stress and to pinpoint any emergency treatments needed. This will also give you some information you can relay to your veterinarian when making medical decisions.

1. Is the animal unconscious? This may be due to a variety of reasons - starvation, dehydration, head trauma, poisoning. Try to find the underlying cause and treat for shock.

2. Is the animal having motor difficulty or paralysis? Reasons may be due to being hit by a car and having head or spine trauma, diseases such as distemper,

3. Are there broken bones. You may need to schedule an Xray with your vet.

4. Are the gums a normal color? Gum color can give you a lot of information. Bright red gums may indicate infection, pale gums internal bleeding or poisoning.

5. Is the animal cold? Neonate animals can't thermoregulate (make their own body heat) and rely on mom to warm them. Warm baby animals slowly before rehydrating.

6. Breathing: Is breathing normal for the species? Labored, shallow, or raspy breathing may indicate health concerns.

FULL EXAM AND TREATMENT

So now you have some important information. You have a brief medical history of what happened to the animal. You have done an inbox exam to confirm species and gather some basic information.

Next, you did your brief exam and have more information which will lead you to develop a plan of action. Next, put the animal in a quiet, dark warm place for anywhere from five minutes to an hour.

Letting the animal de-stress, a bit is important because many animals will die from stress. At this time, you can put in a call to your vet if you need guidance on how to proceed or need to schedule an appointment. You can gather your supplies to begin treating the wild animal.

You will then be ready to start a more thorough exam and treatment.

At this time, I weigh them because that is the first step to giving fluids or medicine. Many many wild animals, especially babies, come in dehydrated. This is the time to give fluids. Read our blog article on administering Fluids.

I also take the time to listen to the heart and lungs to make sure I don't hear fluid or infection. Palpate the abdominal region.

After you give fluids try to stimulate the animal to urinate or defecate.

What you do during the next steps will depend on the circumstances.

WILDLIFE TRIAGE CONSIDERATIONS

MINIMIZE PATIENT STRESS

The first step is always to minimize patient stress. You are not going to eliminate stress. The fact is that the animal does not relate to your petting, cooing words, or efficient medical treatment as a domestic animal would. Just our very presence is going to cause the wild animal to be afraid.

Don't be like the finder who cme into my center cradling an adult groundhog and telling me she (the groundhog) just loves her. Or the human who brought in a coyote with a broken leg and was making kissy noises in their face. These animals are severely stressed and in shock.

There are many things you can do to help the animal be less stressed.

- Keep the talking to a minimum
- Don't have on music or television
- Minimize handling
- Don't allow pets and other animals to be near
- Have a dedicated admitting/triage area
- Allow them to be in a dark, quiet place

EUTHANASIA

We must balance suffering with the probability that the animal will be able to live a normal life and be released. Or possibly have a quality life as an educational animal.

I know this is hard and honestly something I have struggled with. I just don't want to give up. However, euthanasia is not giving up - it is releasing the animal from its suffering.

Renée Schott, Medical Director, and Senior Veterinarian, of the Wildlife Rehabilitation Center of Minnesota (WRCMN) has a fabulous online presentation on wildlife triage located on the Lafaber

Vet Resource site. The video uses several case studies and gives lots of good information.

This video also has a RACE credit option. It's free. You watch the recorded webinar, take a test, and voilà! I took it and can apply one CE credit to my veterinary tech or wildlife rehabilitation education.

REVERSE TRIAGE

So, in the human hospitals, ER nurses prioritize life and death situations. We often do this in wildlife triage as well. Consider Reverse Triage.

In reverse triage, we treat the least ill first. By treating the least ill first we are setting them up for recovery and release. Our job is to try to get the animal to a point where it will be able to live a natural life.

We must acknowledge that we have a limited number of resources - money, time, supplies, staff - all of these play a factor in what we can do. So, the argument can be made that we should use our resources on animals with the best chance of a positive outcome.

What happens when we stretch our limits and our resources?

Quality of care diminishes. Animals don't get the best care, they are overcrowded, and lack sufficient medical care. In addition, humans get tired, cranky, and suffer from compassion fatigue.

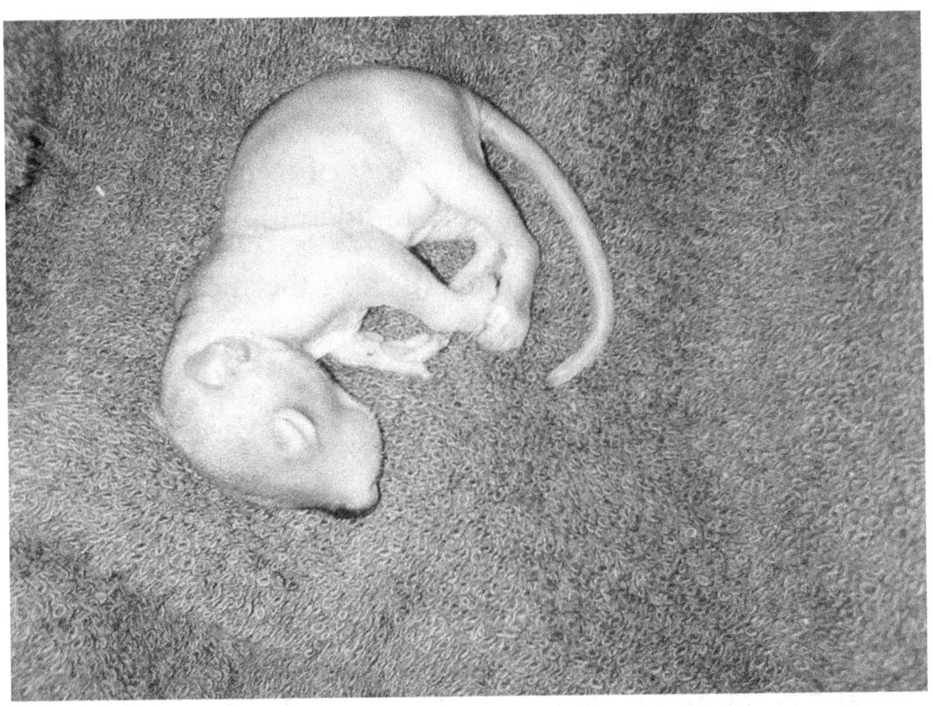

HEAT

Sometimes the first thing you notice when you find or admit a baby is that it feels cold. Cold and unresponsive. Warming the baby is the first important step in saving its life.

Our bodies are made to run at a certain temperature. For humans that's 98.6, for fawns it's 101 and for opossums, it's 95 degrees Fahrenheit. Babies who are neonates, stressed, injured, and/or dehydrated will often experience a drastic drop in body temperature.

THERMOREGULATION

To thermoregulate means to produce heat. Most of us can generate our own heat. Our bodies maintain a consistent temperature.

Neonates, babies with their eyes still closed, can't thermoregulate. They depend on a mom critter to keep them warm. They need additional heat.

PROVIDING HEAT

It's up to us to provide that heat until the babies start thermoregulating. The babies should have a surrounding temperature between 85 - 90 degrees. Older babies and even adults may need to be kept warm if their health has been compromised or they are injured.

Caution is needed when giving supplemental heat. A neonate or other animal that can't move should never be placed directly on the heat source. They may become overheated and unable to escape the heat source.

You can place newspapers or towels over the heating pad. I typically place the infant in a knitted pouch and place them just off the heating pad. Then I keep a thermometer in the carrier or cage to monitor the heat.

For a baby who is mobile, place a heating pad on low under one-half of the carrier. Then the baby has the option of crawling on or off the heated area.

METHODS OF HEAT

There are several methods you can use to add supplemental heat. You may have several of these methods going at any given time to meet the needs of various babies.

HEATING PAD

The heating pad is the most commonly used way to offer heat. They are relatively inexpensive and easy to find. You can just place the heating pad under the container you are using and turn it on low.

I like the Marunda brand just because it's made for pets and has a couple of nice features such as chew-resistant cords and a wipe-off surface.

When you purchase a heating pad make sure you get on without an automatic shut-off. More and more have these as a safety method but it makes it very inconvenient for us.

Heating pads do need to be monitored to make sure they are putting out consistent heat. You will also need to make sure the baby is not too hot or too cold.

PROFESSIONAL INCUBATOR

You can purchase the same incubators that are used in hospitals for neonate human infants. The disadvantage is that they are very expensive. However, many rehabbers feel they are worth the price.

Incubators are easy to use and offer a nice consistent heat. Many of them also allow you to regulate the humidity as well.

To purchase you can raise money through your Facebook page, use the Baby Warm crowdfunding website, put one on your Amazon list, or ask your local hospital for a donation of one. You can also qualify for store credit with Amazon and get them on a payment plan.

PORTABLE AND TEMPORARY OPTIONS

There are many good portable and temporary options. You may choose to use one to warm up a baby before an exam. They are also good if you are transporting baby animals. I sometimes use them for babies who may appreciate some extra warmth but are physically thermoregulating on their own.

Ceramic Disks are my favorite form of temporary heat. Just put them in the microwave to charge them. The heat lasts several hours however you do need to monitor them carefully. Snuggle Safe is my favorite brand for ceramic heaters.

In a pinch, you can heat up a bottle of water and wrap it in a dishtowel. This works well if you are transporting an animal to a rehabilitation center. Make sure the bottle can't roll around onto the baby.

Hot water bottles are something we don't see as often anymore but they are quite handy for emergencies and transportation. They are more stable than a water bottle and hold the heat longer.

HEATING LAMPS

There are many kinds of heating lamps available on the market. Some are made for baby birds, and some made for reptiles. They are made to work with glass aquariums.

I use the reptile ones for turtles that come into rehabilitation. The ones made for reptiles are nice because they can just set on the wire tank covering. You can also get them with clamps that are fixed to the side of the tank.

Heating lamps have several disadvantages. It can be hard to maintain the correct temperature and they are not very efficient. Heat often escapes through the top of the enclosure. Also, they can be a fire hazard if they come in contact with cloth or bedding.

I like the ZooMed brand because they have a sturdy design and I have dropped more than one light fixture! These are the lights I use for turtles and snakes.

Supplies

Getting supplies together for your wildlife rehabilitation facility is very important. You will want to put some thought into how you set up your facility.

Supplies include cages, bedding, food, cleaning, and intake materials. There is always a long list of things that are needed. Your needs may change as you grow or decide to specialize.

SPACE

You may be working from a room in your home, a garage, or a dedicated building. Either way, the first step is to access your space and what species you can adequately care for.

Each species will need a dedicated space and enclosures that meet their individual needs. Animals grow and will require some natural outside space before being released.

A great guide is the Minimum Standards For Wildlife Rehabilitation. It gives enclosure size requirements for many species.

CAGES AND ENCLOSURES

The size of the cages is going to depend on the species and how old they are. Keep in mind that the animal will grow and need to be bumped up to the next size cage. I typically have a three-step system. Neonate enclosure, grow-out cage, and outside pre-release area.

For neonates, you can use glass aquarium-style tanks, plastic tubs, cat carriers, or cardboard boxes. I like to use cardboard boxes for eyes closed babies and glass tanks when eyes open. In the case of the boxes, they can be broken down for trash or recycling. Glass tanks are easy to clean and disinfect.

Many people use plastic tubs. I have concerns about how well they can be cleaned. In addition, plastic can absorb odors and microscopic parasites.

Throwing away a plastic tub for me is hard because it's a waste of resources. So, for me, there's always a balance of finding materials that are sustainable and ones that promote good health and safety.

Cat carriers are another option. I get frustrated with them because they can be harder to open and extract the baby from.

Also, as babies grow, they can and will escape through the door. I once had a whole litter of possum babies climb through and take a self-guided tour of the nursery.

GROW OUT PENS

Grow out pens are larger cages that allow the baby more movement. Movement helps them to grow physically and mentally. I have used a variety of styles from wire dog cages to rabbit hutches to larger cages from the pet industry.

I love the Ferret Nation/Midwest cages and I keep several outside year-round. They are sturdy and stand up to young raccoons' shenanigans! My oldest one is seven years old and is just now having some rust issues around the hinges.

PRE-RELEASE ENCLOSURES

When your baby has grown past the baby stage and is becoming a juvenile you will move them to a pre-release enclosure. They need a bigger space to allow them to start practicing becoming an adult. Climbing, hunting, foraging – these are skills you want to provide for your babies.

You can use a manufactured cage, or you can build a custom cage. I like to use the standard chain link dog kennel and add a top and bottom to make it secure.

BEDDING

Fortunately bedding – blankets and towels- are easy to get second hand. Just let all your friends and followers know that you can use them and ask for donations.

Along with bedding goes washing. It's always advisable to get a second washing machine for animal laundry. Your furry friends do carry a number of parasites and diseases that you would not in your personal wash.

FEEDING

There is a lot that goes into feeding your babes. Fluids, formula, cream are all things that baby mammals may require. As they get older you may add fresh fruits and vegetables, baby foods, and then on to worms and mice.

Keep in mind that if you intend to raise a carnivore such as a fox you need to be dedicated to feeding them live prey foods. It is crucial for them to learn how to hunt as juveniles before they are released.

For supplies, you should be well-stocked on a variety of bottles, nipples, and syringes. There are many options. I use a mix of things.

Some options such as the pet nursing bottles are easy to get at local feed stores. They are inexpensive and come with several nipple options.

For tiny babies, I love the miracle nipples that were developed by Christina Clark, a squirrel rehabber, and the owner of Chris's Squirrels and More. Miracle Nipple fits on the end of a strange and makes it very easy to measure how much the baby eats.

As babies get bigger or for bigger species, I use just generic human bottles because they are very cost-effective. These work well for raccoons and young fawns.

CLEANING

Cleaning involves keeping your work and animal areas clean and free from germs. You may need to have on-hand mops, sponges, buckets – whatever you need to wipe down countertops and clean other surfaces.

Gloves – keep several boxes of nitrile or latex gloves on hand. They are important for protecting both you and the animal.

Disinfectant - Cleaning solutions that will kill bacteria and viruses are important to have around. Try Rescue or a Clorox-based solution.

Masks - Initially, masks were not on my mind as something you should have in stock. However, after experiencing the COVID-19 Pandemic, masks should definitely be in your supply cabinet. Masks are not just for protecting yourself. They are for protecting your babies. Many state Fish and Wildlife and Department of Natural Resources have asked rehabbers to wear masks to prevent transmission of COVID or any other disease to wildlife.

HEAT FOR TRANSPORTATION

If your center offers transportation and picking up babies, you will want to have some options for warming a baby. This is in addition to having your car's heat on and putting them on a warm seat.

Snugglesafe ceramic heaters are great. In fact, I use mine on a regular basis as they can hold the heat for six hours. You just put them in the microwave and heat them for several minutes. You do need to wrap them in a cover (they come with one) or a towel to protect the baby.

Air-activated hand warmers, rice bags, and hot water bottles are all options. Make sure the heat source is not in direct contact with the baby.

OFFICE SUPPLIES

Even if you are just taking in a few squirrels, you will need office supplies. At the minimum, state permitting offices will require you to complete some paperwork.

A computer and printer will make your life much easier.

If you are doing a business, you will want to have an internet connection so that you can promote yourself via social media. Getting a website is a smart idea so that you can be located easily by finders in your area.

FLUIDS

One of the most lifesaving skills you can have in wildlife rehabilitation is the ability to assess hydration levels and give fluids. Dehydration will kill an animal faster than a lack of food.

The process of rehydration begins after warming the baby for thirty to sixty minutes.

WHAT IS DEHYDRATION

The basic answer is that dehydration happens because more water and fluids leave the body than enter it. Simple.

The animal's body an average 75% water. A neonate may be as much as 90% water.

Losing water that is not replenished is a BIG deal.

CAUSES OF DEHYDRATION

Many things can cause dehydration in an animal. Things such as hot weather, no water source, diarrhea from illness, or blood loss.

The most common source of dehydration that we see in babies is from lack of milk. Whether mom is dead, sick, or injured the baby is unable to nurse.

SYMPTOMS OF DEHYDRATION

You can diagnose dehydration by looking at an animal. Some common symptoms are:

- poor skin elasticity
- shrunken appearance especially around eyes.
- lethargy
- dry mucus membranes
- fast but weak pulse

In addition, animals can become dehydrated when they are under our care. Always monitor your baby's intake and outtake. Yes, be obsessed with how much they poop and pee! Some center reasons for dehydration are:

- Medicine and illness
- Formula is not the right consistency.
- Feedings are not on the right schedule for age and species.
- Lack of water source

WHAT IS REHYDRATION?

Rehydration is giving the animal fluids so that you can restore the lost water.

NEVER FEED BABY UNTIL AFTER REHYDRATION

This is very important. Baby animals should never be offered food until after they are rehydrated. Food, and formula is food, can actually cause their system to shut down.

Many times, finders inadvertently kill baby animals because they automatically want to feed them. If you are a finder, call a wildlife rehabilitator or your veterinarian to access what the baby needs.

Even an animal that seems perfectly hydrated should receive fluids to help them transition to new foods. I give everything fluids to start with.

For those of you that have taken the Basic Class with IWRC, you may remember the conversion charts.

When figuring the amount of fluids needed you will consider that fluids are needed for daily body maintenance; for rehydration of lost fluids, and the replacement of fluids lost to excretion, sweating, etc.

Dr. Anne Fowler BVSC, in her presentation for the National Wildlife rehabilitation conference, states that she assumes a 10% loss of fluids as a general guideline, but the animal may have more. I think this is great advice.

The standard maintenance requirement of most species is approximately 50-60 ml/kg/day, or 5% of body weight.

Dr. Fowler states that it is typical that most animals come into your facility with at least a 10% dehydration. This means the total volume of fluid that we give to the baby includes both the "ongoing maintenance requirements and the replacement required from dehydration".

So, in the following example, we assume 50% of this deficit is replaced in the first twenty-four hours and the remainder over the following two days.

- Day 1: maintenance (5%) + rehydration (5%) = 10% of body weight
- Day 2: maintenance (5%) + rehydration (2.5%) = 7.5% of body weight
- Day 3: maintenance (5%) + rehydration (2.5%) = 7.5% of body weight

Fluids are easy to metabolize in the body, can reduce the effects of shock, and helps the body transition.

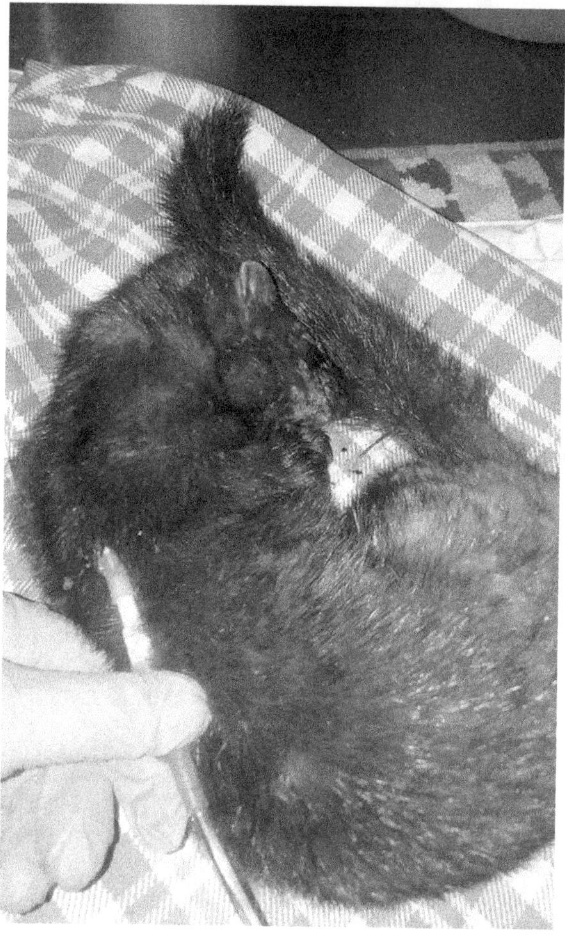

HOW DO YOU GIVE FLUIDS?

There are several methods you can use to rehydrate. The method you use will depend on the health of the animal and the type of fluid you are using.

ORALLY

This method works well if the baby is conscious and alert. Using a syringe and a nipple you can give warm fluids via the mouth.

This method is less stressful on the animal as it's natural for them to take in liquids via the mouth. The fluids will enter the digestive system and get distributed in the body quickly.

Don't use the oral method if the animal is unconscious, has neurological symptoms, or is having seizures.

Tube Feeding is another oral method. Tube feeding is a skill that needs to be learned from a vet as it can cause death if done improperly. Some animals such as opossums are good candidates for tube feeding.

Some good oral fluids are Pedialyte and Gatorade. Both are easily available. Pedialyte is more expensive but can be used in all levels of dehydration. You should get unflavored Pedialyte as it has less sugar.

Gatorade and other sports drinks are good for mild dehydration. I will often mix Gatorade and Pedialyte. This cuts down on the sugar but still flavors the Pedialyte a bit so that they eagerly drink it up.

Lactated Ringers Solutions or Saline solutions can also be given orally. LRS requires a prescription or to be purchased from your vet.

SUBCUTANEOUS

Subcutaneous means under the skin and is often referred to as SubQ. A needle is inserted just under the skin and the fluid is inserted via a syringe or a drip line. This is an easy technique to learn from a veterinarian or experienced wildlife rehabilitator.

If an animal cannot or will not take fluids orally then the subcutaneous method is the right option. This method is not quite as fast-acting because the fluids need to be absorbed by the body.

In a serious dehydration case, you may choose to use both methods to have maximum benefits.

Lactated Ringers is the brand most often used in veterinary and medical offices. IV solutions require a prescription. I typically buy the Ringers from my vet.

You can also purchase from Chewy or KV Supply with a prescription from your vet.

STEPS TO REHYDRATING A BABY

Give the baby a quick exam and access their medical needs.

1. Warm the baby
2. Determine the level of dehydration and decide the method of rehydration
3. Weigh the baby and determine the amount
4. Warm the fluids to body temperature
5. Give initial fluids

Depending on age and species you will continue to give fluids every two to three hours for the first 24 hours.

Continue to assess baby vitals and monitor for improvement.

SWITCHING FROM FLUIDS TO FORMULA

After 24 hours of fluids, you can start to make a slow switch to formula. This process is slow to allow the baby to adjust to a food source.

Also, don't forget to keep giving replacement fluids until the baby is properly hydrated. You can still continue SubQ fluids while switching to formula. You can also choose to add the replacement amount of fluids to the feeding schedule.

When switching to formula make slowly. For the first two feedings use 1/4 formula and 3/4 fluids. Feedings three and four will get 1/2 formula and 1/2 fluids. Feedings five and six will receive 3/4 formula and 1/4 rehydration fluids. After that switch to full strength formula.

Observe the baby to make sure they are properly digesting each mixture and having normal toileting before moving on to the next level.

FORMULA

As a licensed wildlife rehabilitator, you are charged with feeding your babies until they are ready to be released. This can be a daunting task. There is a lot of controversy among experts when it comes to what is the best formula to give.

Feeding is going to vary greatly based on the species and age of the baby. This is why as rehabbers we have to be Jacks/Jills of all trades. It is important to understand the needs of every species you choose to take in.

I have a YouTube Video Wildlife Rehabilitation Basics: Nipples and Bottles that you can watch that gives an overview of feeding equipment.

MY BEST ADVICE

So, my first bit of advice is to listen to the experts but to most of all closely observe your babies. By experts I mean established rehabbers that are experienced, speak at conferences, write research papers, ect. Don't listen to every yahoo on Facebook.

Ask yourself:

- Are they gaining weight steadily? Weigh them every couple of days when they are small and record the data.
- Are they active and exploring at an age-appropriate level?
- Do they appear sick or weak?

Any of these may indicate that the formula is not meeting the needs of your babies. Talk to your veterinarian or an experienced wildlife rehabber to decide what changes should be made. Don't use a wait and see method with tiny babies – it may be too late when you decide to make a change.

Know your species. I'm constantly surprised when rehabilitators don't know what the needs are of various species. Wild animals have higher metabolisms and so have different nutrient requirements than your puppy or kitten.

Fox Valley has some great information on their website about these requirements. You can make a simple spreadsheet and hang it on a bulletin board.

WHAT FORMULA IS BEST?

This is the million-dollar question.

There are several brands of formulas that are commonly used. The most recommended brands are PetAg and Fox Valley. Both these companies have done testing to ensure their products can meet wildlife needs. However, you need to follow the recommended ratios.

PetAg is a large corporation that produces a variety of brands including Esbilac, KMR, Multi-Lac Milk, and Zoologic. One nice thing is that they have a frequent buyer program where you can earn free products.

Fox Valley is headquartered in Illinois and sources local fresh milk to manufacture its products. Fox Valley designs and makes formulas for exotic animals such as wildlife as well as pets. Fox Valley has specialized formulas for almost every wild animal you can imagine. This is great, especially for those species that have specialized nutrition needs such as beavers, bears, and moose.

GOAT MILK

Esbilac Goat Milk or "real" goat's milk is sometimes used by rehabbers especially if an animal is showing allergy symptoms. However, most rehabilitators do not recommend goat's milk. In her book, Wild Mammal Babies, Irene Ruth, does not recommend using goat's milk and states that goat's milk is too low in protein and fat for most species.

Remember because wildlife has higher metabolism their need for fat and protein is much higher.

MIX AND MATCH

Should you just buy one type of formula and give it to everyone? NO

Your various babies will all have different nutritional needs. You will have a variety of formulas at your center. In my experiences, I have given the skunks Esbilac, the squirrels get Fox Valley, and the fawns get multi-lac.

Now, this does get a bit complicated. Some rehabbers will mix Esbilac and Fox Valley formulas when feeding a particular species. This may be done to provide optimum levels of nutrients, or it may be done to cut costs.

HOW MUCH FORMULA?

Every species will vary but there is a basic rule of thumb. Weigh the baby using a gram scale. The stomach capacity is generally about 5% of the body weight.

Divide the total body weight by 5%.

For example, if a baby weighs 100 grams then 5% of that is 5ml's. We use cc's or ml's to measure the fluid. After you mix the formula, you just draw up the correct amount into a syringe that nicely has the levels marked on it.

WHAT ARE CC'S AND ML'S?

CC stands for cubic centimeter. ML stands for millimeter. They are just two ways that are used to measure volume in the metric system.

CC and ML are interchangeable. When you look at your syringe you want to pay attention to the number – not whether your unit says cc or ml.

MASS MARKET FORMULAS TO AVOID

There are a number of formulas that have been produced for the puppy and kitten market that do not meet the needs of wildlife.

According to Irene Ruth DO NOT USE Hartz, Mothers Helper, Nurtural, or other like brands.

HOMEMADE FORMULAS FOR WILDLIFE

Please don't use homemade formulas for wildlife. I don't care if you have raised a hundred baby squirrels on Mamaw's homemade puppy formula. Studies have shown that deficiencies as babies can cause issues later in life.

Homemade formulas aren't balanced based on what that species needs and may not work. Nutritional-related problems such as MBD and Angel Wing often take months to manifest themselves. You may have released the baby and think everything is wonderful.

PUTTING SUPPLEMENTS IN THE FORMULA

Sometimes wildlife rehabilitators will add supplements to the formula. They do this because they feel the baby needs something a bit "more". In some cases, health issues may be a reason.

You may also talk to rehabbers who start adding things to prepare the baby for transitioning to solids.

Yogurt, applesauce, and human baby cereal are all things that may be added. Vitamins can also be added.

In general, it is felt that if you are using a good quality formula and feeding the correct amounts then you don't need to add things to the formula. The above foods can all be used as transition foods for babies who are merging to solids.

Vitamins and herbal supplements are things I have used with animals who are having health issues. They may have come in emaciated or with wounds. It's done on a case-by-case method and never takes the place of regular feedings.

Probiotics are another commonly given supplement that can be added to the formula. Bene-Bac is a good brand that I have used. Fox Valley makes one called LA200.

Talk to your veterinarian if you have questions about health and nutrition.

COLOSTRUM

I consider colostrum a supplement. Colostrum is the pre-milk, or first milk produced by mammals when young are born. Colostrum contains a high level of nutrients as well as antibodies. It helps protect the newborn from diseases.

Colostrum is also a mild laxative that helps to stimulate the digestive system and waste elimination. In addition, it increases the beneficial microflora in the digestive tract.

Newborn or neonate babies may benefit from having colostrum added to their formula. I like Wholistic Pet's brand from Amazon. You can purchase bovine colostrum at places like Tractor Supply or your local feed store.

CARE OF FORMULA

Formula is perishable and needs to be treated like food. Store it in a cool dry location. The nutrients in the formula may decrease when it is exposed to hot and or humid weather.

Buying formula in bulk is very cost-effective, however make sure you can store it properly. The cost savings don't help if you get to the bottom of the barrel and the formula is of poor quality.

You should make enough formula for 24 hours and then store it in the fridge.

MIXING FORMULA

Formula needs to be mixed well and allowed to settle so that the air bubbles dissipate. You can use a food processor or blender to combine ingredients well.

They also make mixer bottles that people use for sports drinks that contain a wire whisk ball. When you shake up the water and formula the ball mixes them together.

Add formula to warm water so that it dissolves better.

PetAg recommends you refrigerate powdered formula after opening for up to three months.

KEEPING FORMULA WARM

Keeping the formula warm during feeding can be tricky as it cools off in the syringe quickly. You can have warmed water available in a bowl to set your syringes in. You can also use a human baby bottle warmer or a slow cooker.

BUT SOMEONE ON SOCIAL MEDIA SAID...

There is always a lot of crazy and untrue information floating around the various social media channels. This is no different for wildlife rehabilitation.

Don't get information from a social media platform. I have done a search a couple times for people in prominent social media groups. Turns out they weren't even listed or licensed wildlife rehabilitators in their state. They are simply people that like to talk and get satisfaction commenting on social.

If you hear an influencer or guru giving information message them personally. Build relationships with other rehabilitators in your area so that you can learn and grow together.

FEEDING EXPENSES

Wildlife rehabilitation is a costly endeavor. Feeding expenses are a large chunk of the wildlife rehabilitators' budget.

Many people do not realize that wildlife rehabilitation is a "volunteer entity". Most monies to feed and house the baby wildlife that is rescued come from finders, donors, and the pockets of the rehabbers themselves.

Whether you are a finder or a rehabilitator it is important to understand the costs of wildlife rehabilitation. For most people feeding and purchasing formula is the biggest expense.

For others, it is veterinary care. Caging, housing, and electric (heating) are all considered. In addition, most rehabbers must pay permit fees and take education classes to get their license.

This chapter will focus on feeding costs as that is a foundational expense for any animal. Very little has been written about the actual cost breakdowns which I think hinder our progress as a business. Choosing what brand of formula is another topic! Over the past couple of years, I have asked established wildlife rehabilitators for their thoughts.

As baby animals get older, they need more natural foods. For herbivores, this can help keep costs down if you have an organic yard or field from which to gather plants. You can also raise insects as a food source.

*** My research may not reflect current inflation!

WHY IS THIS IMPORTANT FOR FINDERS?

Finders are the critical first step in the wildlife rehabilitation process. In my experience, finders are kind and compassionate people who want to help animals. However, they often do not understand the day-to-day demands of rehab or why they are asked to donate money for helping.

When a neonate baby comes into a rehabilitation facility it is essentially helpless. The first thing it needs is a warm safe place. Fluids, formula, and natural foods will help it grow. In addition, depending on the circumstances, the baby may need medical intervention.

COST OF RACCOONS AND WILDLIFE REHABILITATION

Raccoons are among the most popular and the most expensive animals to rehabilitate. Raccoons are a long-term investment for a rehabber.

Depending on their age of admittance, they often stay the allotted time (6 months in Kentucky). Raccoons need a lot of "training" as in the natural world their mother spends a great deal of time teaching them survival skills.

My estimate is that raccoons cost about $225 per kit to feed them to the release stage.

The Wildlife Center of Silicon Valley (WCSA) in California estimates that they spend $40 each week for twelve weeks for every raccoon they take in. So $480 per raccoon for formula and an omnivore transition diet.

An Arizona Wildlife Rescue spends an average of $1000 per four kits so roughly $250/kit.

RABBITS

Sure, baby bunnies are tiny. But they still need regular meals and a high-quality diet.

Stephanie Carlson of St. Melangell's Small Animal Sanctuary outside Cincinnati, Ohio states that her baby rabbits' cost $120 in formula alone over 60-90 days.

SQUIRRELS

For WCSV baby squirrels average $240.00 from neonate to release (about 12 weeks). This includes formula, rodent block and whole foods as the squirrel grows.

Stephanie Carlson says that a litter of four baby squirrels take approximately 120 days before they are ready for release. That is about $165 in formula and nuggets. Carlson uses Fox Valley formulas.

BIRDS OF PREY

Birds of prey are voracious eaters. Not only that, they need fresh (often living food) for a healthy diet and one that teaches them to hunt.

Mario Nickerson runs Nature's Edge Wildlife and Reptile Rescue in the Dallas, Texas area. Nickerson handles birds of prey at his center.

He told me (via Facebook) that he broke it down for a local rehabber this way:

Whole quail cost us $1.40 each

Mice vary between pinkie to adult $0.15 to $3

Rats vary between pinkie to adult $0.25 - $6 each

A 2-pound bag of frozen mixed veggies is $1.94 (typically one bag per day feeds 4-8 animals depending on species)

"I'm usually feeding more or less 10 adult raptors, from Kestrels to Redtail Hawk size. Costs me $500 to $600 a month, just maintenance diet".

The WCSA website states that predatory Birds (Raptors) cost about $50/week per fledgling.

"Cost of caring for an injured adult bird of prey can be quite expensive – from $250 to upwards of $2,000 or more depending upon the length of stay. Rehabilitation can last 4-6 weeks, though some birds can stay as long as one year (such as in electrocution cases). Raptors eat a carnivorous diet – a barn owl can consume up to 10 mice per day!" (WCSA, 2017)

The Chattahoochee Nature Center in Georgia, focuses on resident animal care, public education, and rehabilitation. They have several educational birds of prey.

Bald Eagles cost $3000/year and Great-horned Owls cost $2900/year to feed. These of course are adult animals who are non-releasable.

On their website they state that "the average cost of wildlife rehabilitation care" is:

- One raptor: $50/week
- One reptile: $20/week
- One amphibian: $10/week

COST ANALYSIS STUDIES

There have been few cost analysis studies in the field of wildlife rehabilitation. One study was done in Catalonia, Spain between the years 1995 - 2013. The study looked at feeding expenses as one aspect of the overall treatment and cost benefits.

The study looked at the average cost of the species which included things other than feeding, determining amphibians and tortoises to be the most cost-effective.

Ironically most animals in this study (40%) came into rehabilitation due to government confiscation. The study remarked how there is still a high incidence of animal kidnaping in Europe.

Orphaned young were 32% of the study.

Vaccinating wildlife in rehabilitation programs and in their natural habitat is a controversial topic. Wildlife rehabilitators may receive conflicting information from their state officials, wildlife biologists, and their veterinarian.

Your state Department of Fish and Wildlife may tell you to do one thing and your veterinarian or board members another. To complicate matters, we give wildlife vaccines off-label, meaning they are not legally cleared for use on wild animals.

In addition, vaccines are an added expense for wildlife rehabilitators. Many rehabbers may be comfortable giving shots however many states require a veterinarian to actually give the rabies vaccine.

This is an important conversation to have. In this blog, we will discuss these topics, mention some views from other rehabilitators and discuss ways to prevent disease.

I asked about wildlife vaccines in a Facebook Wildlife Rehabilitation group so I would have some diverse input. I received responses from several leaders in the wildlife rehabilitation community and share some of their responses.

WHAT CAN WILDLIFE REHABILITATORS DO TO PREVENT DISEASE IN THEIR CENTERS?

*** Note: Volume 2 of this series will go deeper into the topic of diseases, parasites, and wounds.

Vaccines are used as one way to prevent diseases and their spread among populations. Young humans and domesticated animals get vaccinations on a regular basis. They are one tool we can use to prevent the spread of many diseases.

Invariably, we bring in animals that carry diseases. Wildlife rehabilitation is about caring for sick, injured, and orphaned animals. Not the healthy one who is doing well.

If we look at the big picture, however, there are many things we can do to keep our animals healthy. Here is a list of non-vaccine things you should be doing to prevent disease.

- Work with your vet to develop an intake and treatment protocol.
- Keep wildlife separate from domestic animals.

- Have a quarantine area for incoming animals.
- Keep areas clean and sanitized.
- Always wear gloves and other PPE.
- Keep good records.
- Try to lower stress to improve health. (Yours and the animals!)

Why Vaccinate the Wildlife in Your Center?

Elena Rizzo, a licensed wildlife rehabilitator at Into the Wild in New York and a researcher for Animal Help Now, gives three powerful reasons to vaccinate.

1. Outbreak protection for your facility

2. Provides our patients better chances for survival in the wild

3. Protects domestic animals and public health."

Let's look at each one.

OUTBREAK PROTECTION

The sad truth is anywhere we place animals in close proximity to one another there is a chance for disease spread. We saw this happen with human populations during 2020 and the COVID pandemic.

Similarly, some species such as raccoons and deer may have large populations in your area. Wildlife biologists often use this reasoning to dissuade rehabilitation practice for "common" animals. However, the root problem is often a lack of or extinction of large predators.

Centers have had highly contagious diseases such as distemper and parvo spread rapidly among young animals. Knowing what diseases are in your local wildlife populations is critical to developing a plan to help your animals.

In addition, keeping up with wildlife rehabilitation best practices through your local, state, or national group is advantageous.

PROVIDES YOUR PATIENTS WITH IMMUNITY

Wildlife rehabilitation is all about saving an animal's life so that they may be released back into the wild.

The goal of immunization is to increase the animal's ability to fight the disease and to slow disease transmission among a population. They keep the animal from suffering and increase their quality of life.

Several people on Facebook commented on our investment. As wildlife rehabilitators, we have a lot invested in these animals. Time, energy, and money – often money from our own pockets. Not to mention sweat and tears.

Sheri Hanes Meade, of TLC Wild Baby Rehab, Inc., is a licensed rehabber and leader in Indiana. She aptly makes the comparison "if you do not vaccinate it would be like playing Russian Roulette with your baby's lives. Animals Shelters vaccinate. We should be no different."

COMMUNITY AND PUBLIC HEALTH

There is a lot to be said about the importance of public health. The act of wildlife rehab brings populations of animals and humans together.

Wildlife in today's world lives in close proximity to humans. Urban wildlife is on the rise. Vaccines have proven to be a way to manage and control many zoonotic diseases.

WHAT ARE ZOONOTIC DISEASES?

Zoonotic diseases are those diseases that can be passed from animals to humans. Rabies is probably the most famous zoonotic disease. The Bubonic Plague was given stardom during the Middle Ages and is still with us today. Others include Salmonella, Leptospirosis, and Roundworms. These diseases come in the form of bacteria, parasites, and viruses.

Interestingly there is also a reverse zoonotic disease where humans can make their pets ill. Examples of this are Staphylococcus aureus (MRSA), H1N1 influenza, and the more recently coronavirus. In 2020 coronavirus was passed from zookeepers to animals in their charge most notable tigers at the Bronx Zoo.

Zoonotic diseases are a public health concern that affects everyone in the community. European countries have been much more proactive in this area than we have been here in the USA. In part possibly because their communities are much older and established with a high incidence of urban wildlife.

Vaccination of wildlife in rehabilitation centers, as well as vaccination programs aimed towards wildlife in public parks and urban areas, has helped to reduce the occurrence of many zoonotic diseases.

In fact, rabies among foxes has been nearly eliminated in thirteen European countries In Europe, it is not unusual to have foxes living in urban areas.

Rabies used to be considered a public health threat in countries such as Germany and England. An aggressive program using trap/vaccinate/release and oral rabies vaccination (ORV) over the past twenty years has been very successful.

RABIES IN US WILDLIFE

According to the CDC, 92% of rabies cases came from wild animals. Specifically, bats, raccoons, skunks, and foxes, in descending order. The USDA works with the US Department of Fish and Wildlife to distribute rabies vaccines among wildlife populations in high-risk areas.

While Kentucky has not been considered a high-risk area, Oral Rabies Vaccination (OTR) has been dropped along the Virginia border to stop the spread of the raccoon variant more prevalent in the Appalachian Mountain region. Dr. Joanne Maki stated the goal is to "establish herd immunity within a rabies reservoir species. Doing so reduces virus transmission in wild animals, while also reducing the risk of rabies virus exposure in domestic species and humans".

DISADVANTAGES OF VACCINES IN WILDLIFE

To be fair, I did have a couple of people on social media say they do not vaccinate wildlife in their programs. There are several disadvantages to vaccination.

Probably the most cited disadvantage is the cost. Vaccines are expensive. In some states, including Kentucky, only a licensed veterinarian can administer the rabies vaccine. These costs can add up quickly.

In addition, juveniles can be hard to catch and handle to administer a vaccine. We do raise them to not want human contact!

Also, it should be noted, we often think of rabies vector species, deer, and groundhogs, when planning to give immunizations. Many people who do squirrels and or bunnies do not vaccinate those species as they are not as high risk. However, that would geographically vary.

VACCINATION SCHEDULES

Controversy also exists on how often and with what variant to vaccinate with. Raccoons and foxes can be tricky because both the canine and feline variants may be necessary.

What diseases you vaccinate for may also reflect your geographic location and what is present in your environment. For example. Distemper in wildlife is a big problem in my area. So, we feel distemper and rabies are the most important vaccines to give. To be clear we use the 5-way shot so Canine Distemper, Adenovirus Type 2 (CAV-2 cross protection CAV-1), Parainfluenza, and Parvovirus Vaccine (MLV) are all covered.

Vaccination schedules are somewhat arbitrary and often reflect older laws meant to contain diseases. There is no evidence that animals, including our beloved cats and dogs need annual boosters throughout their lives. Studies have suggested that two shots lead to adequate antibodies. We give them boosters to make sure they are protected and to adhere to state regulations. The rabies vaccine is legally required in the state of Kentucky for dogs, cats, and ferrets.

According to Merck's Veterinary Manual "Individual animal and vaccine variability make it difficult to estimate the duration of protective immunity"

Vaccines are not licensed for wildlife and there are few established administration schedules. Sadly, wildlife does not meet the need for funding for these studies. When we administer inoculations, it is with the understanding that it is "off label". More research is certainly needed in this area, not only for wildlife but as an assurance for quality public health.

Talk with your vet about what vaccine schedule to use. There are several good resources.

Vaccines Have Been Critical in Saving Endangered Species

Another advantage to vaccinations is it helps species who are at risk due to low populations. Endangered animals have been saved by populations receiving immunizations. The Black-Footed Ferret is an example of an endangered species that recovered successfully in part due to a vaccination program.

The Black-Footed Ferret is susceptible to a variety of the plague they got from eating prairie dogs. In addition, distemper had lowered the population which was close to extinction. A controlled breeding program and vaccination schedule allowed the successful reintroduction of thousands of healthy ferrets in native prairie ecosystems.

In addition, due to the risk of mustelids to their population, the Black-Footed ferret has also been given the COVID vaccine.

Resources

International Wildlife Rehabilitation Council

www.theiwrc.org

Phone 866.871.1869

A non-profit based in Eugene, Oregon that serves rehabbers all over the world. At the time of this writing membership is $30.00/year

Their vision – "We envision a world where the conservation and welfare of wild animals is well served by an effective symbiotic relationship between wildlife rehabilitators and other wildlife professionals."

The IWRC provides online, onsite courses as well as webinars. They have a professional journal available for members. IWRC hosts a job board and animal placement board. In addition to their Basics Course required by many states they offer a Certified Wildlife Rehabilitator certificate.

National Wildlife Rehabilitator Association

www.nwrawildlife.org

(320) 230-9920

A non-profit based in Bloomington, Minnesota that serves wildlife rehabilitator primarily in North America however their vision is "The National Wildlife Rehabilitators Association and wildlife rehabilitation as a profession are recognized and respected worldwide." Membership is $65 a year for the individual.

The NWRC offers a symposium every year that is held in a different location each year in the US. Members also receive their publication the peer-reviewed journal Wildlife Rehabilitation Bulletin. They offer small grants and scholarships – check their website for current projects.

Animal Help Now app

https://ahnow.org/

Animal Help Now is a resource for finders and rehabbers. Finders can use an app on their phone or use it on desktop to put in their address and find out what licensed wildlife rehabilitators are near them. Wildlife Rehabilitators can get listed with them. AHNow also has a number of resources on the website.

Supplies

Amazon

Amazon carries a wide range of supplies used by wildlife rehabilitators.

Chris's Squirrels and More

https://www.squirrelsandmore.com/

Located in Connecticut, the owner Christina Clark has been a wildlife rehabilitator since 1994. Chris designed and developed the Miracle Nipple, a product I highly recommend. Her store offers a variety of supplies and foods for wildlife in rehabilitation.

Henry's Pets

https://henryspets.com/

Located in Floyd, Virginia Henry's offers supplies for pet and wild squirrels as well as small rodents and other domestic pets.

Help With Setting Up a Website, Promotion, or Social Media?

Contact Ame Vanorio at Fox Run Writing Services

foxrunwritingservices@yahoo.com

About The Author

Ame Vanorio is an organic farmer, environmental educator, and wildlife rehabilitator. She was raised on a traditional Kentucky farm with horses, cattle, and tobacco. Ame's hands on experience includes:

- 29 years of off-grid self-sufficient lifestyle experience

- 6 years urban homesteading

- Organizing and selling at Farmers Markets, Farm Stands, and CSA

- 15 years in wildlife conservation and licensed rehabilitation work

- 20 years in education

She holds graduate degrees in Education and Environmental Science and is the Founder/director of Fox Run Environmental Education Center.

Fox Run EEC is a non-profit that teaches organic agriculture, green building, and wildlife conservation. Ame is a licensed wildlife rehabilitator and teaches classes in the community and online.

Ame recently moved from Kentucky to Wisconsin to be closer to her son and family. She is focusing more on education projects and helping underserved communities experience nature and gardening.

You can follow us on Facebook, Twitter, and YouTube. Check out my Author Page on Amazon.

www.ingramcontent.com/pod-product-compliance
Lightning Source LLC
Chambersburg PA
CBHW081838250726
48659CB00008B/2499